RED

BLUE

POO

ALISON MARCELINO

Archway Publishing books may be ordered through booksellers or by contacting:

Archway Publishing
1663 Liberty Drive
Bloomington, IN 47403
www.archwaypublishing.com
844-669-3957

Because of the dynamic nature of the Internet, any web addresses or links contained in this book may have changed since publication and may no longer be valid. The views expressed in this work are solely those of the author and do not necessarily reflect the views of the publisher, and the publisher hereby disclaims any responsibility for them.

Any people depicted in stock imagery provided by Getty Images are models, and such images are being used for illustrative purposes only.
Certain stock imagery © Getty Images.

ISBN: 978-1-4808-9944-5 (sc)
ISBN: 978-1-4808-9945-2 (hc)
ISBN: 978-1-4808-9943-8 (e)

Print information available on the last page.

Archway Publishing rev. date: 11/25/2020

RED

BLUE

POO

RED

BLUE

POO

UP

DOWN

BROWN

IN

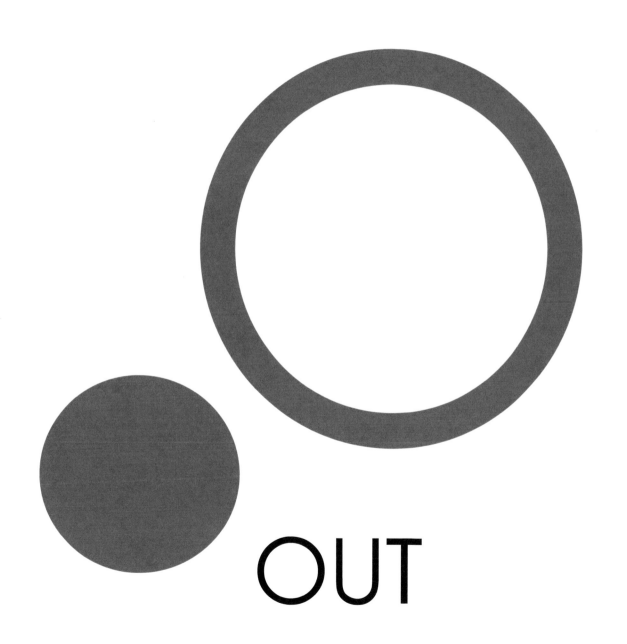

OUT

SPROUT

BEE

TREE

FREE

YELLOW

CELLO

FELLOW

GREEN

CLEAN

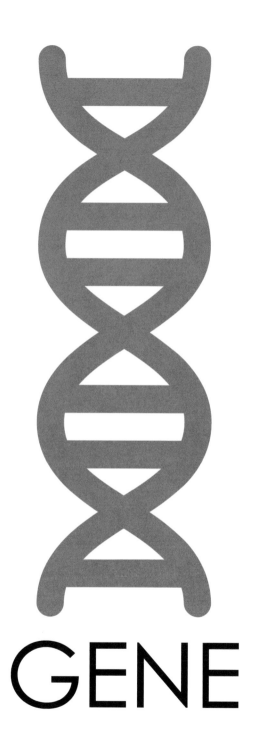

GENE

YOU

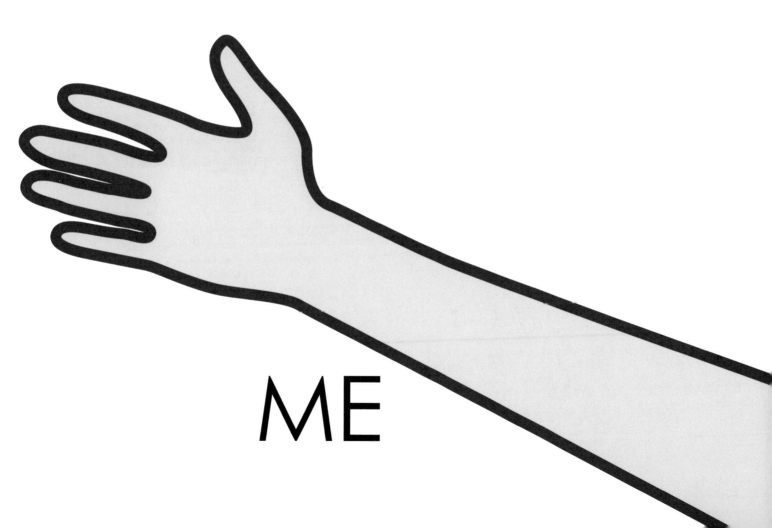

ME

WE

Printed in the United States
By Bookmasters